FRIENDS
OF ACPL

PRINTCRAFTS
for Fun and Profit

Seymour Fleishman

Albert Whitman & Company, Chicago

Copyright © 1977 by Seymour Fleishman
Published simultaneously in Canada by
George J. McLeod, Limited, Toronto
All rights reserved. Printed in U.S.A.

Library of Congress Cataloging in Publication Data

Fleishman, Seymour.
   Printcrafts for fun and profit.

   1. Copying processes—Juvenile literature.
2. Printing—Juvenile literature. I. Title.
Z48.F56   686.2   76-48907
ISBN 0-8075-6633-0

Contents

Printcrafts—getting into print 4
Copying machines 6
Gelatin duplicators 8
Stencil duplicators 11
Offset printing 15
Project 1/ Invitation or greeting card 17
The money part 20
Useful art supplies 21
Using clip art 23
Project 2/ Bookmarks 24
Project 3/ Letter folders 28
Project 4/ Personal stationery 30
Lettering sheets 32
Using lettering sheets 33
Ornament and border sheets 34
The great clip art treasure hunt 35
Project 5/ A newspaper, magazine or newsletter 36
Project 6/ Books 44
Project 7/ Calendars 48
Project 8/ Advertisements 48

Printcrafts—Getting Into Print
(And making money, too)

Not long ago all kinds of printed matter—newspapers, booklets, greeting cards, posters, notices, advertisements—were produced by professional printers and artists. Now it's different. There are new materials and ways of printing. Using them, you can get into the fascinating world of printcrafts.

You can be a designer who makes posters, cards, and stationery for your own use and to sell. You can be a publisher of a school or club newspaper, of a neighborhood or church newsletter. You can put out a joke book or a small magazine. You can also be an editor, a writer, and a reporter—or you can concentrate on designing and getting printed what someone else has edited, written, or illustrated.

When you're into printing, you're also on the way to being a business person. You deal with printers, you buy supplies, and you sell your product or your service. This means keeping records of your costs and setting fair prices. When you earn money, you can buy new supplies and tools. With work and imagination, you're really in the business of printcrafts.

In each printing process, the most important step is making your design or master copy in the way that works best. In these pages, you will find easy directions for different kinds of printing, what to do and what not to do. You will learn how to use the simple art supplies most often needed. There will be helpful hints, little tricks of the trade, scattered through this book, too.

Here are the four ways to print which you're likely to use:

1 Copying machines, such as Xerox, 3M, or A. B. Dick

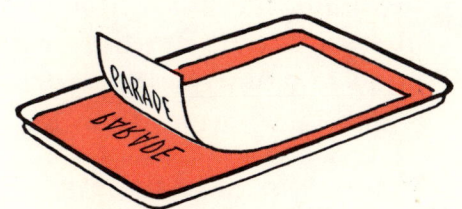

2 Gelatin duplicators, such as the hectograph

3 Stencil duplicators, such as Mimeograph or Gestetner

4 Offset printing, such as Instant Printing, Quick Print

Copying Machines
(for up to 12 copies)

Suppose you have found a lost puppy. If you put up a dozen or so notices in your neighborhood, the pup's owners may see one and claim their pet.

You can draw all the notices by hand, but there is a much easier and faster way. You can make one original and have it copied by a coin-operated machine. These machines are in many places: banks, libraries, post offices, drugstores.

Several companies make copying machines and each may be a little different. But they work pretty much the same way. They copy anything written, drawn, or printed on a sheet of paper which is no larger than 8½ × 14 inches.

You use most of the machines this way:

1. Put the sheet you made face down on the glass and lower the rubber cover
2. Put coin in slot
3. Press the "Print" button
4. In a few seconds the copy comes out

5 If you want more copies, leave the original in place and repeat 2 and 3.
6 When you have all your copies, don't forget to take out your original! (Many people do forget.)
7 Try markers or crayons to add color by hand.

Many business offices have copying machines. If you are lucky, your parent or a friend has one and you can get copies there.

Making the original copy

Make your original copy on a sheet of white paper or cardboard no bigger than $8^1/_2 \times 14$ inches.

Use pen or a black felt-tip pen. You can paste down letters or pictures from magazines or newspapers. Photographs can be copied, but not very well.

Copies from a coin-operated machine are fairly expensive, so if you need more than a dozen copies, the hectograph method on the next pages might be better for you.

Gelatin Duplicators
(for up to 50 copies)

This is the cheapest printing system and the simplest. The printing equipment is just a layer, or pad, of gelatin in a shallow pan large enough to hold an 8½ × 14 inch sheet of paper.

Many stationery or office supply stores sell a hectograph kit for just a few dollars. If your store doesn't have a kit, you can make your own this way:

gelatin-glycerin-water mixture

Put 2 ounces of unflavored powdered gelatin in a bowl. Add 6½ ounces of water. After an hour, add 7¾ ounces of glycerin (sold in drugstores).

Put some salted water in the bottom of a double boiler and empty the gelatin mixture in the top pan. Heat the mixture for 30 minutes, stirring occasionally. Pour into a cookie or cake pan with low sides and of the right size. Let the mixture set.

Making the master

Get a few sheets of duplicating carbon paper from the stationery store. It comes in purple, red, green, blue, and black. The purple makes the best copies.

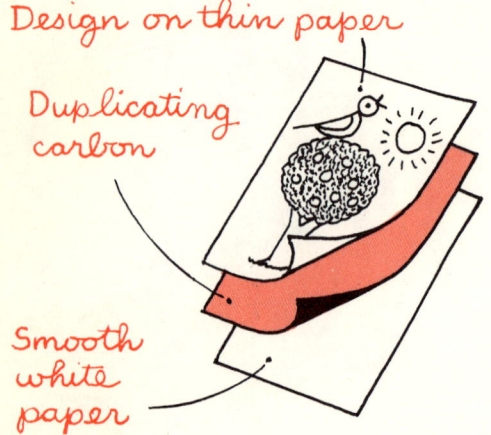

Design on thin paper
Duplicating carbon
Smooth white paper

On tracing paper or other thin paper, either 8½×11 or 8½×14 inches, make your design in pencil or ink. Next, put a sheet of carbon paper, carbon side down, on a sheet of smooth white paper, such as duplicating, typing, or mimeo paper. This should be the same size as your design. Place your design on top of the carbon and tape this "sandwich" to a smooth hard board or table.

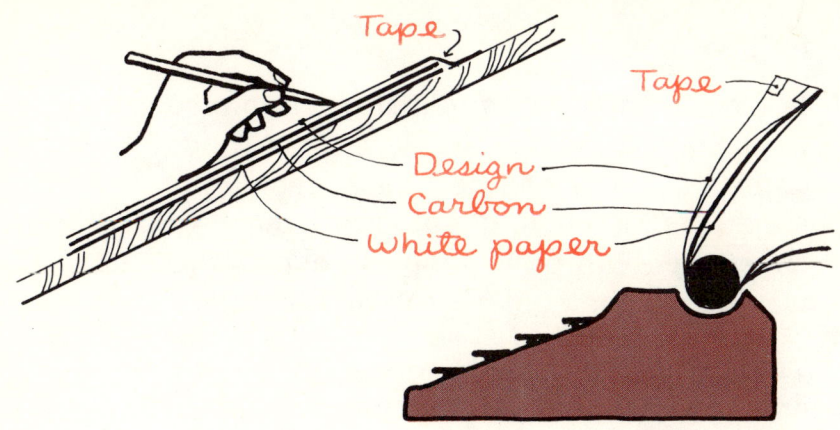

TRANSFERRING THE MASTER

Moisten pad

Remove extra water

Master, face down

Design is now on gelatin pad

With a ball-point pen, firmly trace your design. If you want part of your design in another color, change carbons, being careful not to shift the design or master sheet underneath.

If you wish, you can put the "sandwich" in a typewriter and type parts of your design.

Separate the sheets. Your design is now transferred to the bottom sheet. This is your "master."

Transferring the master

Sprinkle a little water on the gelatin and spread it around with your hand. Let the gelatin absorb the water for five minutes, then blot up the extra water with a sponge and sheets of clean paper.

Now put one end of your master on the gelatin and gently lower the sheet, smoothing out any bubbles with your free hand. After two minutes carefully lift off the master. Your design is now transferred to the gelatin.

GELATIN DUPLICATORS

Printing

Lower a sheet of duplicator or mimeo paper on the gelatin. In 15 to 30 seconds some of the ink will be transferred to the sheet. Lift it off and put down the next sheet. You can print about 50 copies this way before the copies become too pale.

When you are finished, moisten the gelatin and cover it with a piece of plastic wrap. In a day or two the ink will have sunk to the bottom of the pan and your hectograph is ready to use again.

Besides carbons, some stores sell hectograph pencils and inks which you can use directly on the master.

Gelatin prints are useful for newsletters, invitations, and so on, but the color is usually not strong enough for posters. If you need more than 50 copies, or stronger and blacker printing, try the next two methods.

Spirit duplicators

Prints from a spirit duplicator machine look like hectograph prints. The master is made in a slightly different way. If there is a spirit duplicator you can use, ask an experienced person to show you how.

Stencil Duplicators
(10 to 1,000 copies)

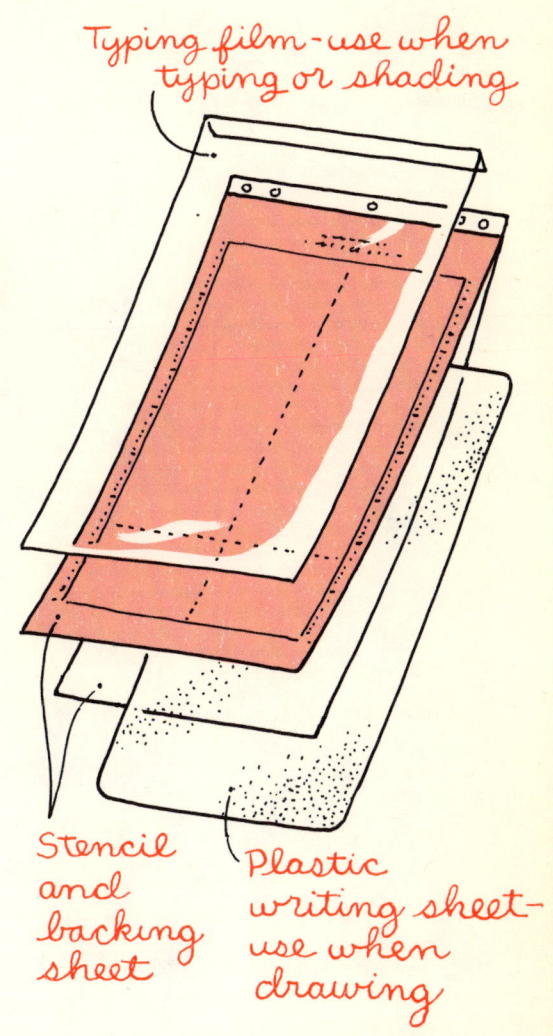

Almost every school, church, or office has a stencil duplicator. It is usually called a "mimeograph," but this name belongs to one company. Other companies make stencil duplicators, too.

You make your design on a special stencil. This is put on the machine, and the ink is forced through the stencil on to the paper.

The stencil

The stencil is a sheet of tissue covered with a waxy coating. Ink cannot get through this coating. If you type on the stencil, or draw on it with a pointed tool, the waxy coating is pushed away from the tissue and ink can get through.

Making the design

Lay out your design in pencil on tracing paper 8½×11 or 8½×14 inches. If some parts are to be typed, type them on the paper.

If you have a headline, draw a dark guideline across the sheet and letter on it.

When you're satisfied with your design, go over everything except the typewritten parts with a felt-tip pen.

Cutting the stencil

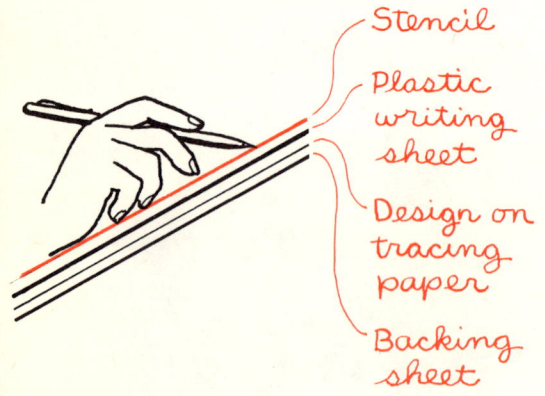

Stencils come in colors, but the easiest to trace through is white.

TYPING. If there is to be typing on your stencil, do that first. Slip your design under the stencil and with a felt-tip pen mark where the typing is to go. (Don't break the stencil surface.) Remove the design and type, following the instructions that come with the stencil.

DRAWING. Make a "sandwich" of the white stencil sheet, a plastic transparent writing sheet, your design, and the stencil backing sheet on the bottom.

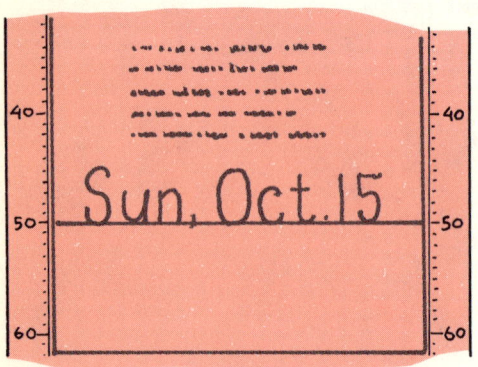

Get your design straight on the stencil by making the headline guideline hit the same numbered lines printed on the edges of the stencil. Hold your design in place by taping it to the backing sheet.

To draw lines on the stencil, you can use a special stylus, but an ordinary fine ball-point pen works very well. Work on a hard smooth surface, such as a glass or wood table top.

You should be able to see your design through the white stencil. With firm pressure, trace over your design. From time to time lift the stencil sheet up to the light and look through to make sure you are cutting a good, clean line. (Practice first on a spoiled stencil to get the feel of it.)

Stencils are quite delicate, so draw carefully, especially where one line crosses another. You can mend tears with stencil correction fluid.

If you must use a blue or green stencil, you will be able to see your design through the dark color if you tape your "sandwich" to a window and do the tracing there.

LETTERING. You can do lettering freehand or you can get lettering guides at the stationery or art supply store.

SHADING. Add gray areas or textures to your design by using a piece of medium sandpaper or window screen. Put the sandpaper under the stencil and a typing film on top. Now rub the ball-point pen back and forth over the area you want to shade.

Printing the stencil

Each stencil duplicator has its own special features, so ask an experienced person to show you how to print your stencil or to do it for you.

POSTER Printed on a stencil duplicator. The original was 8½ x 14 inches.

Sandpaper shading →

Hand lettering

Done with a lettering guide
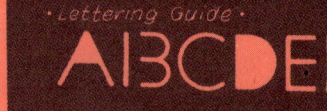

Done on a typewriter

Offset Printing
(100 copies or more)

Copying machines, gelatin, and stencil duplicators can be called homemade printing methods because you do most of the work yourself. But "instant printing" is really professional offset printing, making copies that are sharp and black.

If you know how to use "instant printing" you can make printed items of professional quality at very low cost. The rest of this book shows simple ways to do this.

You have probably seen a shop in your town with a sign reading *Quick Printer, Speedy Print, Instant Printing,* or something like that. If not, use the Yellow Pages of your telephone book, looking under Copying and Duplicating Service or Printers.

This is a new sort of print shop. It can do certain kinds of printing very fast at low prices. A set price list tells you the cost of 100 (or 200, 300, and so on) copies on $8\frac{1}{2} \times 11$ inch paper. Heavier paper, colored paper, or $8\frac{1}{2} \times 14$ will cost a little more. The ink is almost always black, but sometimes colored inks can be had at extra cost.

16 OFFSET PRINTING

To get good printing at low prices that your "instant printer" offers, you must have "camera-ready copy." This simply means that everything is pasted on a sheet exactly as you want it on the printed piece.

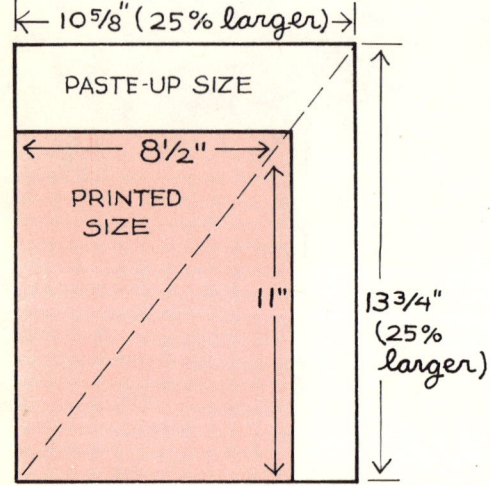

Everything on the paste-up, as it is called, will show up on the printed piece. So you must clean away smudges, fingerprints, or unwanted lines. Type and lettering must be carefully pasted in straight lines. Everything should be sharp and black.

Sometimes it is easier to make the paste-up larger than the printed copy will be. Ask your printer if he can reduce your paste-up and to check the proportions. You can do this yourself by drawing a diagonal line as shown here.

Your printer may want things done a bit differently than the way described here, so talk with him before making your original paste-up. Tell what you want and ask about price. Make sure that the way you plan to work is OK.

In most cases, if you prepare your copy as shown in the following projects, your printer will be very pleased.

Working with instant printing is a way to have fun and make money, too. You can design booklets, programs, greeting cards, posters, and much more. Some of these projects will be suggested here.

PROJECT 1 **An Invitation or Greeting Card**

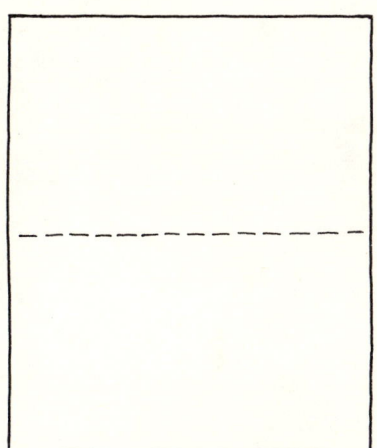

Making the layout

An invitation or greeting card planned as a French fold looks professional. Printing is only on one side of the sheet, but it looks as if it is on both sides.

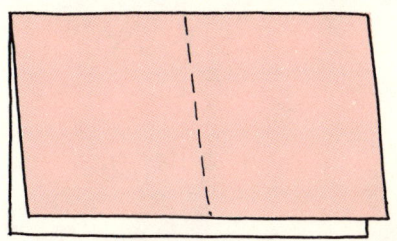 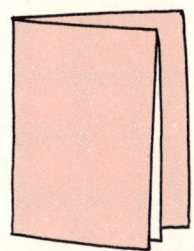

Fold an 8½ × 11 inch sheet in half, then in half again.

Plan the cover of the card and what will appear inside. Put your own name as the designer on the back if you like.

Now unfold the sheet. Follow this layout to make your finished artwork that will go to the printer.

18 PROJECT 1/ INVITATION OR GREETING CARD

Making the finished paste-up

1 On a fresh piece of 8½ × 11 paper draw light blue lines where folds will be. This is your paste-up sheet. Put it aside.

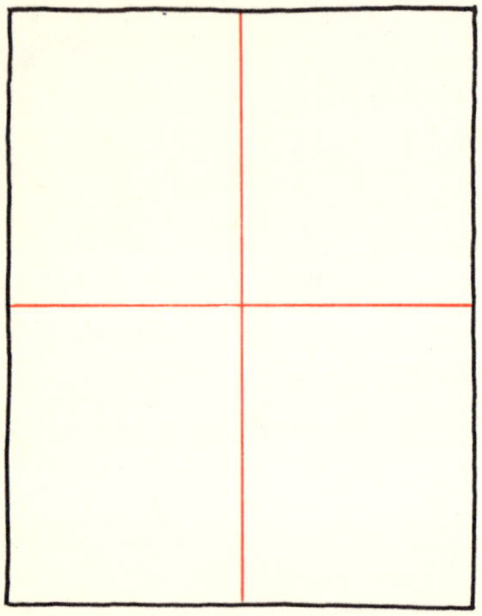

2 On other paper, lightly draw your cover design. When you like it, go over the lines with a felt-tip pen or black pencil. Trim to fit and paste the cover art in the right position on the paste-up sheet.

HELPFUL HINTS

On a scrap of paper with a straight edge make marks for the top and bottom guidelines for lettering and the space between lines. Use this to space lines for lettering.

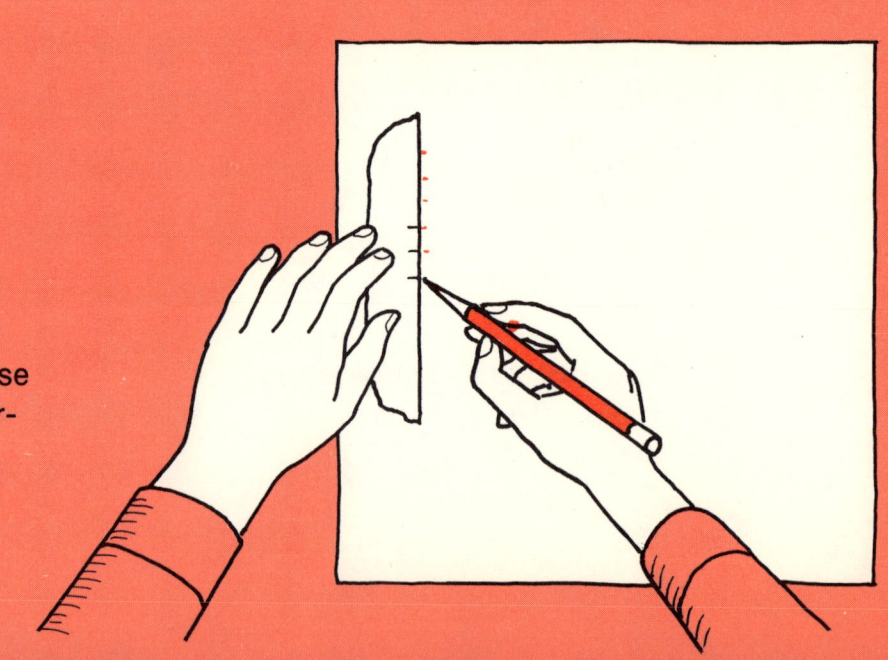

PROJECT 1/ INVITATION OR GREETING CARD 19

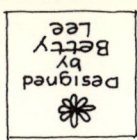

3 Draw guidelines for the lettering. (See Helpful Hints below.) Do the lettering with black pencil or felt-tip pen. Paste in position.

4 Carefully erase unwanted pencil lines, smudges, etc.

5 Take your camera-ready paste-up to your printer. Ask about colored paper if your wish, but don't ask for folding. Do it yourself and save.

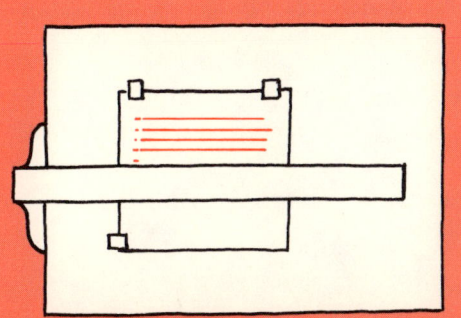

If you have a drawing board and T square, use them to draw lettering guidelines. If not, you can draw them this way.

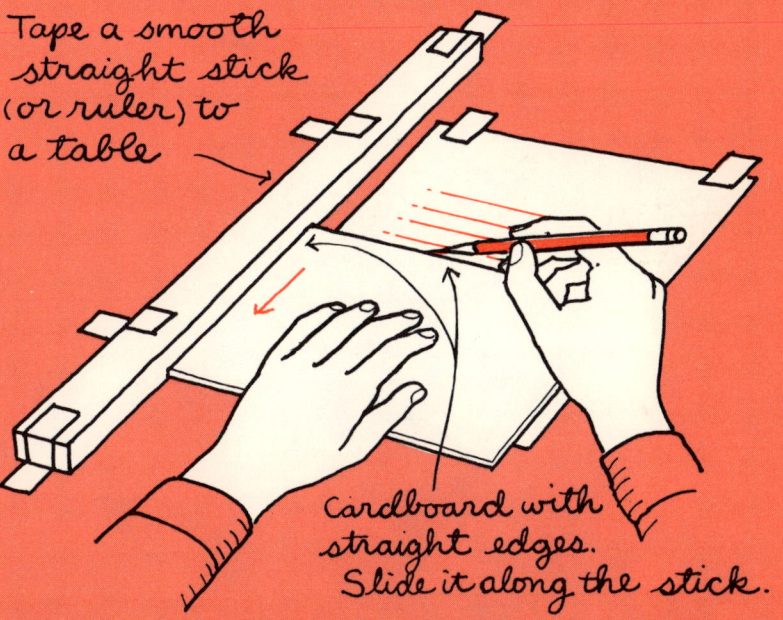

Tape a smooth straight stick (or ruler) to a table

Cardboard with straight edges. Slide it along the stick.

The Money Part

When you make something to sell, add up your costs—for printing and art supplies and envelopes, if you have to buy them. Suppose you make 200 greeting cards. They cost you $7 for printing, $4 for envelopes. If you sell them for 10¢ each, you will make a profit of $9. That pays for your time and some new art supplies. You're in business!

```
Sales
    200 greeting cards at 10¢ each      $20.00
Expenses
    Printing - 200 cards    $7.00
    200 envelopes            4.00
                           $11.00       -11.00
Profit                                  $ 9.00
```

Useful Art Supplies

These are tools you need to make good paste-ups. You may have some already. You can get others in art supply or stationery stores, supermarkets, dime stores, and hobby shops.

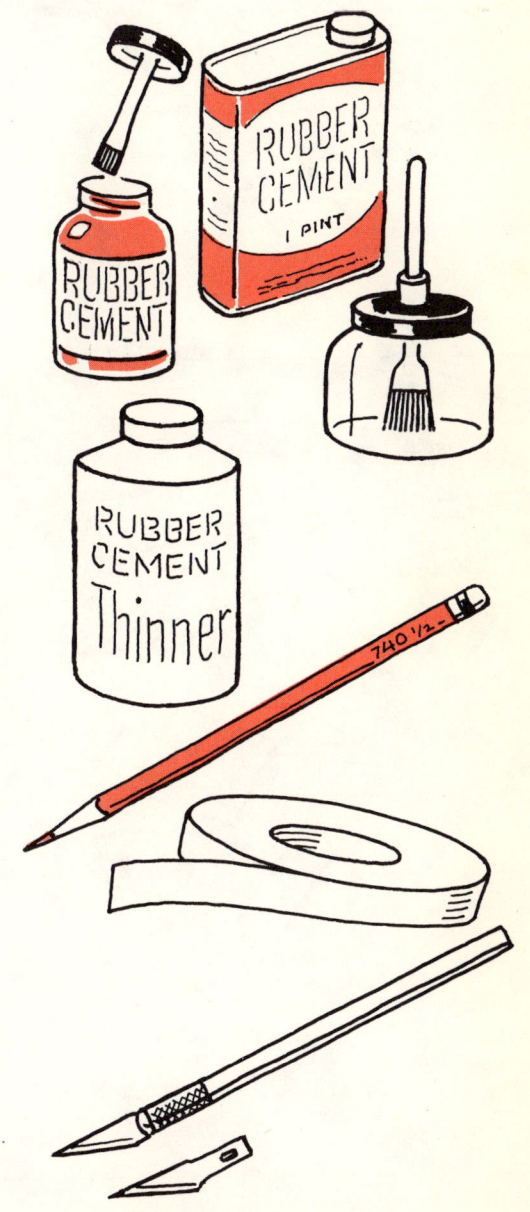

RUBBER CEMENT
   Better than paste, because it doesn't wrinkle paper, and stuck-down pieces can be pulled up and moved. Start with a small can or jar with a brush in the lid. Later you can get a pint can of cement and a dispenser jar. Or reuse the original can.

RUBBER CEMENT THINNER
   For thinning gummy cement and loosening stuck-down pieces.

BLUE PENCIL
   Get a blue pencil such as Eagle Verithin Sky Blue, 740½. Blue lines don't have to be erased because the printer's camera doesn't "see" blue.

WHITE DRAFTING TAPE
   For holding down paper and covering spots, unwanted lines, etc.

X-ACTO KNIFE
   For cutting out paper, etc. The handle holds throw-away blades. Get a package of No. 11 blades.

22 ART SUPPLIES

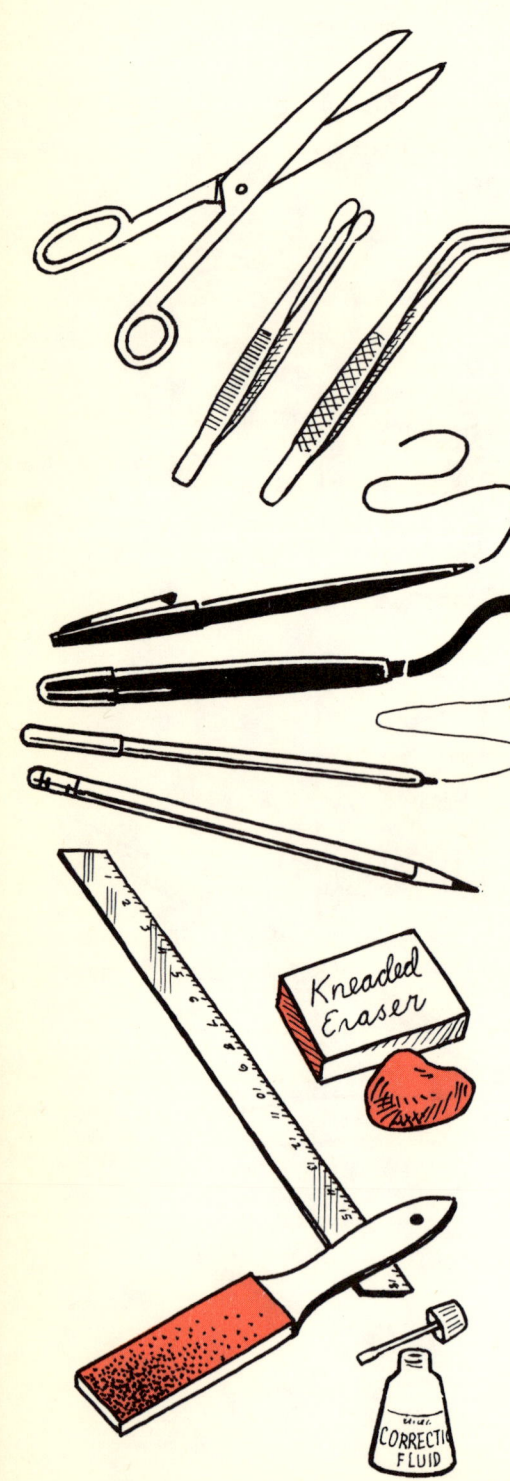

SCISSORS
These should be good enough to cut paper smoothly.

TWEEZERS OR TONGS
Those like a stamp collector's are good for handling small pieces of paper.

FELT-TIP PENS
Black, fine line, for drawing and lettering. Heavier markers for filling in black areas.

BLACK BALL-POINT PENS

BLACK PENCILS
HB or soft lead.

KNEADED ERASER
Less likely to leave dirty streaks.

SANDPAPER BLOCK OR SHEET
Good for sharpening pencils.

RULER
Metal or wood with metal edge.

WHITE CORRECTION FLUID
Good for correcting typing errors, hiding pasted edges.

Using Clip Art

Many professional designers of printcrafts don't draw well. They make beautiful printed pieces by using pickup or clip art. They cut out printed pictures, decorations, borders, and letters to use in their designs. You can do the same.

Looking for clip art is like a game. You'll find useful material in newspapers, old magazines, old dictionaries, old mail-order catalogs, old textbooks (such as botany books). Get the habit of clipping interesting items and putting them in a clip file. Avoid pictures from new books or anything that has a © or "Copyright" on it. Good clip art should be sharp, quite black, not gray. Photographs usually will not print well.

Many of the following projects show how to use clip art.

PROJECT 2 **Bookmarks**

Bookmarks make good gifts. Booksellers like them for advertisements to give away, and your school librarian can use them to interest readers in different books.

You can make five bookmarks on one sheet of heavy colored paper (card or cover stock).

If you use white paper, add color with a felt-tip marker. It's easy and gives your work an attractive look.

HELPFUL HINT

A quick way to divide a sheet (or line) into five equal sections:

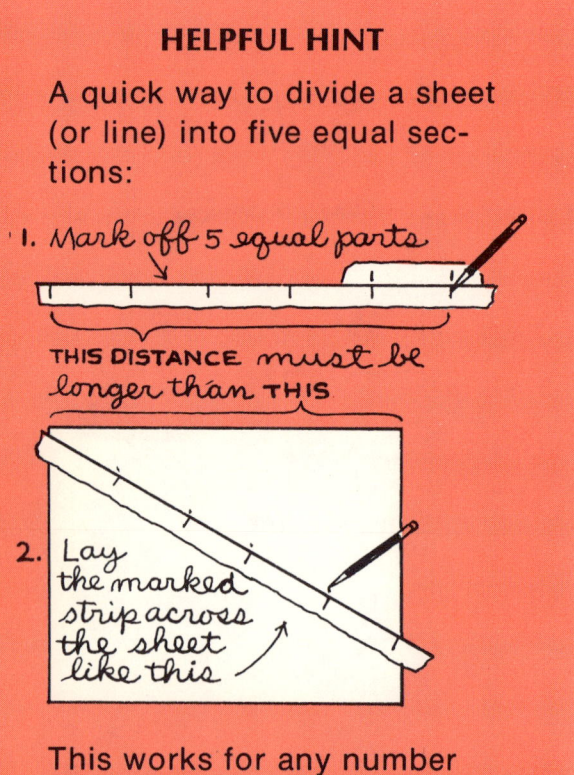

This works for any number of sections.

PROJECT 2/BOOKMARKS 25

Two of these designs come from clip art books—one of plant and flower woodcuts, the other of "catchpenny" engravings from the 1700s. Sometimes you'll use only part of a picture, other times you may combine several different clippings. The third design is a fancy alphabet from a lettering sheet.

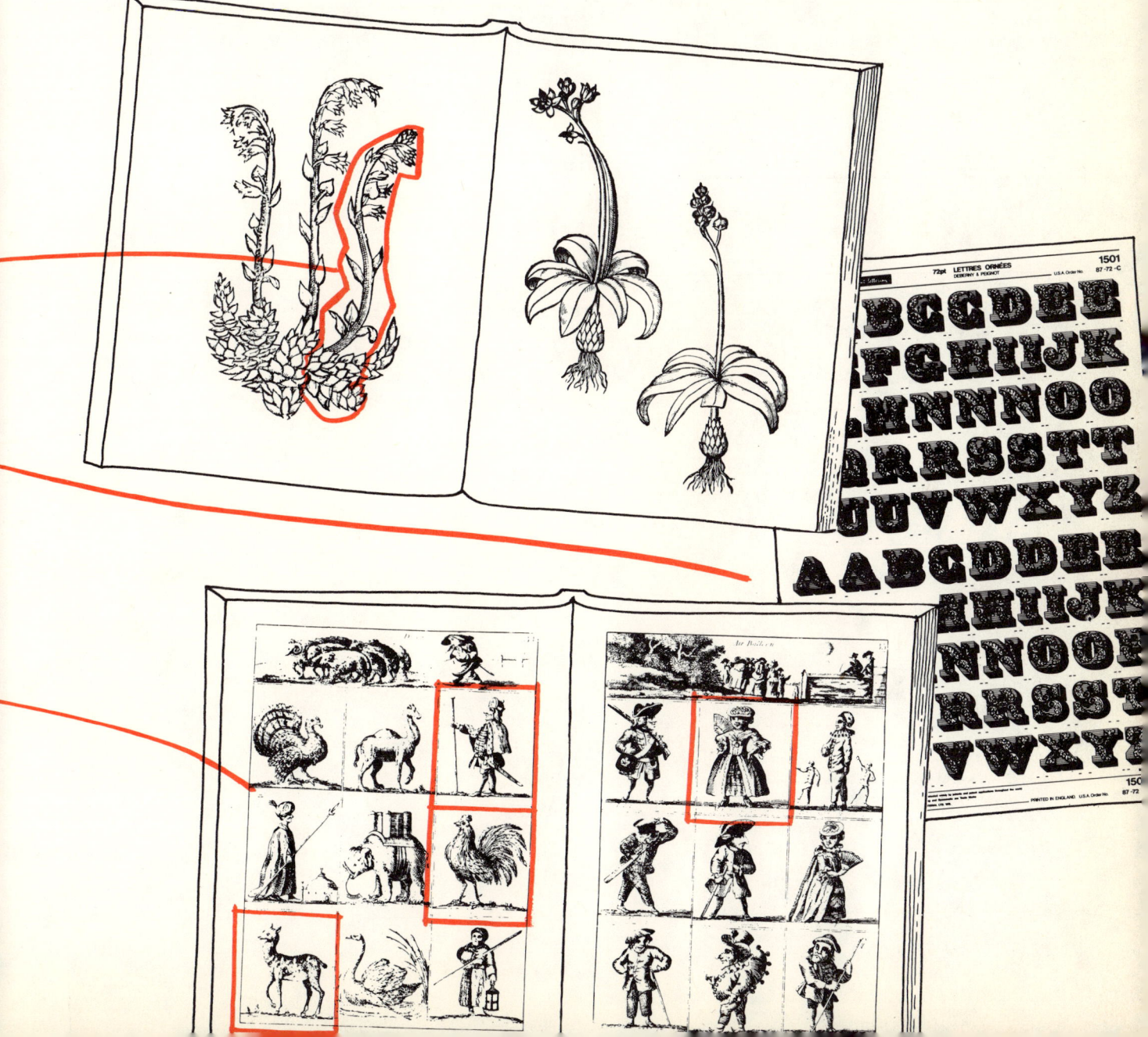

PROJECT 2/ BOOKMARKS

Making a paste-up for your bookmarks

1 Make a paste-up sheet divided into five equal parts. Draw blue lines and black tick marks at the ends of the lines.

2 Cut out clip art and lay the pieces on your paste-up sheet. When you have an arrangement you like, mark the outline with a blue pencil.

Using rubber cement

Place the first piece of clip art face down on a scrap sheet. Coat the back with rubber cement.

Work carefully but quickly. Rubber cement dries fast, but you have time to slide your work into place and get it straight. Use your tongs to keep finger marks off the paper.

Leave a ½ inch margin all around

you can hold pieces in place with bits of of tape or dabs of cement

PROJECT 2/ BOOKMARKS   27

Put a clean piece of paper over what you've cemented down and rub. If some rubber cement squeezes out, let it dry and rub it away carefully with a little ball of dry cement.

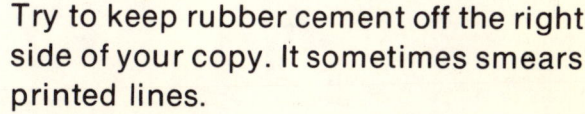

Try to keep rubber cement off the right side of your copy. It sometimes smears printed lines.

When everything is cemented in place clean up any smudges or dirty marks. Now you can head for your printer.

When sheets are printed, cut the bookmarks apart at the tick marks.

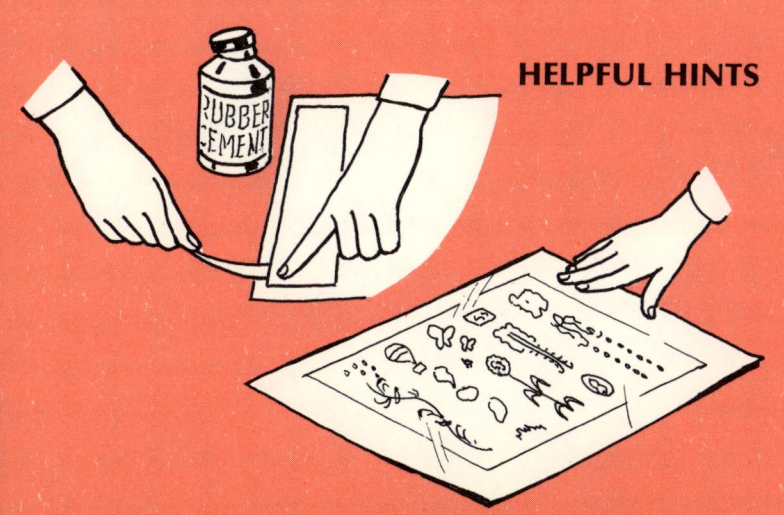

HELPFUL HINTS If an edge or corner is loose, brush cement on both sides of a strip of paper and slide the end under the loose spot. Press down with a clean finger. Remove the paper and press again.

It's easier to see if work is straight if paste lines are hidden. Lay a piece of thin paper or tissue over your work and see how it looks.

Seal with tape or a gummed circle

PROJECT 3 **Letter Folders**

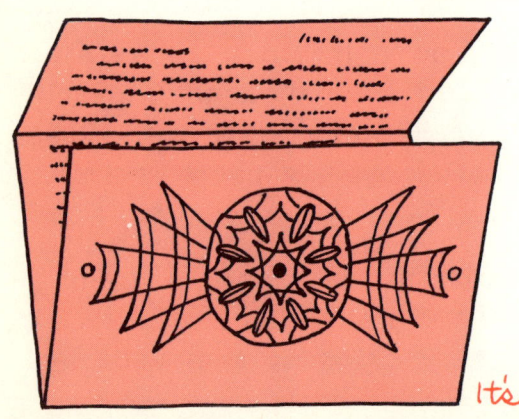

A letter folder is really an envelope and letter all in one. It can be sealed with a sticker or tape.

You will want to have these folders printed on heavier paper, or stock. Some printers have colored paper for an additional cost.

It's fun to invent abstract designs

PROJECT 3/ LETTER FOLDERS 29

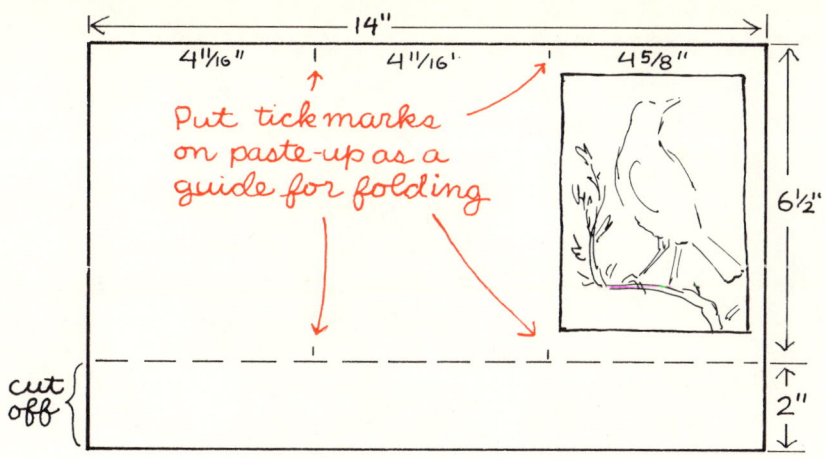

If you use 8½ × 14 inch paper, cut off a strip as shown to give your letter a more pleasing shape.

HELPFUL HINT

If you find heavy paper hard to fold neatly, first score the line with a table knife

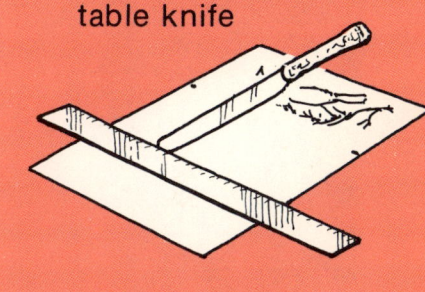

Letter folders are a good item to sell, especially if you personalize them with a drawing of the customer's house, dog, cat, or perhaps hobby. Often you can find clip art that is just right.

PROJECT 4 **Personal Stationery and Envelopes**

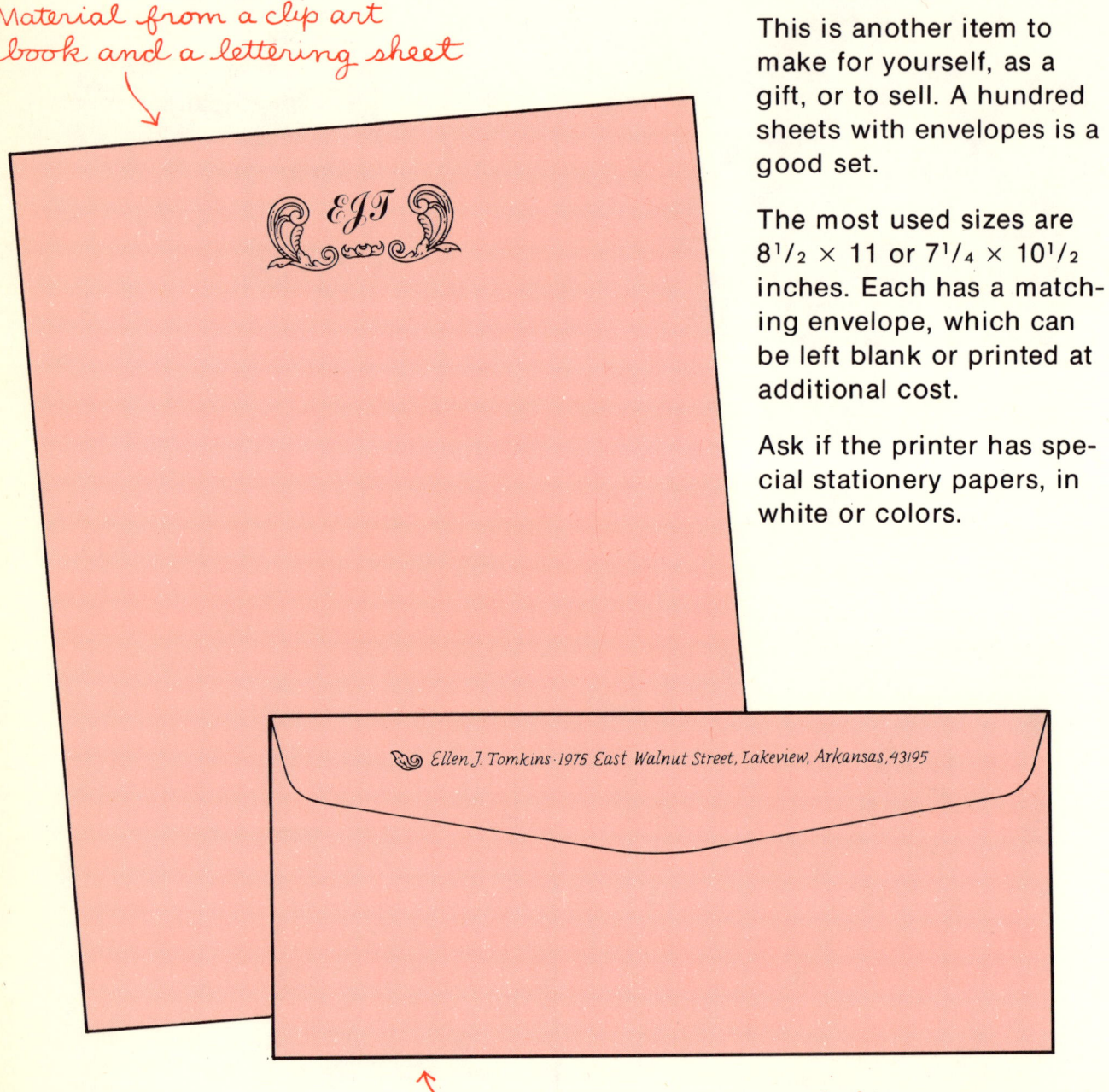

Material from a clip art book and a lettering sheet

Clip art decoration and hand lettering

This is another item to make for yourself, as a gift, or to sell. A hundred sheets with envelopes is a good set.

The most used sizes are 8½ × 11 or 7¼ × 10½ inches. Each has a matching envelope, which can be left blank or printed at additional cost.

Ask if the printer has special stationery papers, in white or colors.

PROJECT 4/ PERSONAL STATIONERY 31

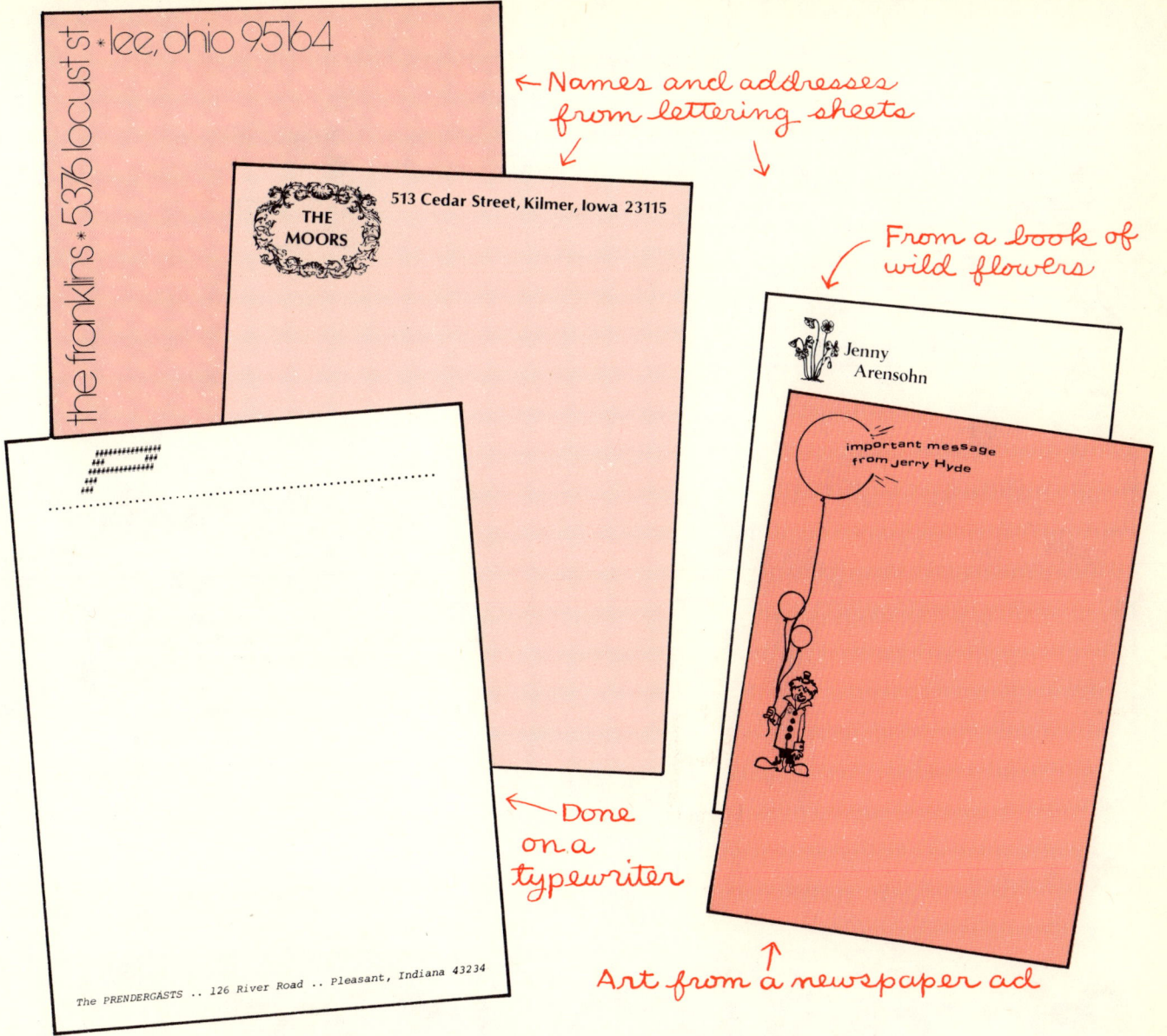

Here are a few of the many designs you can make using readymade art from clip books, borders and ornaments cut from magazines or lettering sheets.

Initials in a fancy border are an easy way to make stationery, but if you want full name and address, you can use a typewriter, especially if it has a special typeface. Or you can hand-letter the address with a fine pen and india ink or use lettering sheets.

Lettering Sheets

These are sheets of thin plastic with alphabets printed on them. Your art supply store has catalogs showing many styles and sizes of type.

Ask if you can have sample catalogs. They have useful information and tips.

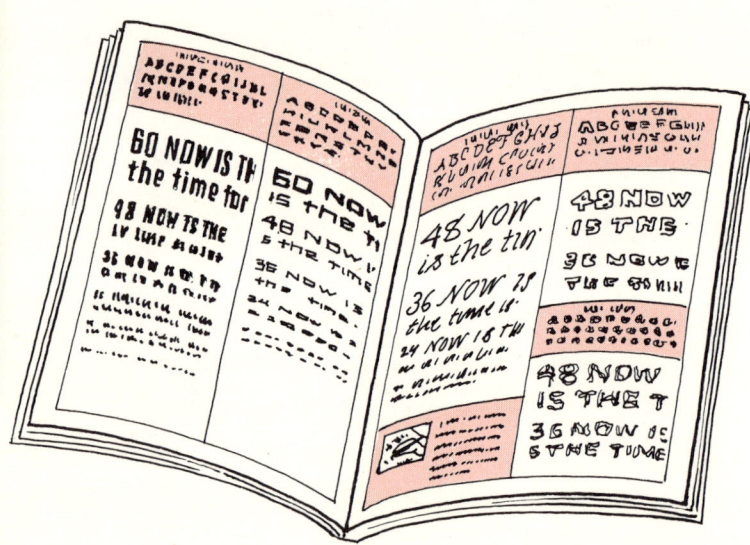

Using Lettering Sheets

There are two kinds of lettering sheets, cutout and transfer.

CUTOUT SHEETS have a waxy coating on the back, and a paper backing sheet.

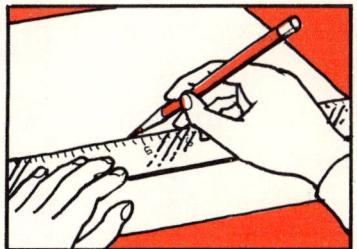

Draw a blue line on a sheet of white paper.

Cut out each letter and the line below it. Don't cut through the backing sheet.

Move each letter to its place, lining up the black line over your blue line.

Cutout letters can be moved around until the spacing looks good to you. Cut away the black base lines, cover the work sheet with tissue, and rub down firmly with fingernail or spoon.

TRANSFER SHEETS have the letters printed on the underside. They have a backing sheet to protect the lettering.

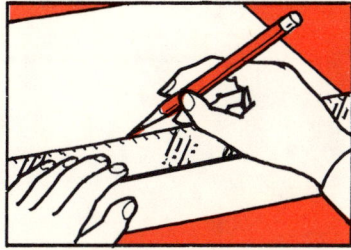

Draw a blue guideline on a sheet of white paper.

Move the whole sheet to get the wanted letter in position, lining up the black line over your blue line.

With ball-point pen rub over the letter. Lift the sheet away. The letter will be transferred to your work sheet.

Ornament and Border Sheets

These are only a few of the ornaments and borders on sheets that work like lettering sheets. This material is like a set of building blocks you can put together in many ways.

HELPFUL HINT

Lettering sheets are expensive for large sizes. Small sheets are sometimes available if you need only a few letters. Try to choose type styles you can use more than once and then build a collection as you earn money to buy more sheets.

The Great Clip-Art Treasure Hunt

Clipped from a book of early advertising art.

Here are samples of the wonderful things you can find in books, papers, magazines, advertising. Sometimes a clipping can spark your imagination, inspiring you to produce an exciting new printed piece.

Remember to clip anything that looks interesting. Put it in your file for future use. If you're going to use a piece of art more than once, make a copy on a good copying machine. You can fill a sheet to duplicate many pieces at once.

1947827

Borders and type from ads in newspapers

Cut from old books, magazines, mail order catalogs

Opening Weus make plan
that has then might be to
 educate yo
AMERICA'S for your re
 improve yo
nationally adough some n

You can trade Whatever your dreams
protection— plans, in most cases s
high leverage them realities. And the

PROJECT 5 A Newspaper, Magazine, or Newsletter

Here's a project that can be as small or as big as you and your friends care to make it. You can do it as a one-time project or go to press weekly or monthly. You can have a 2-page paper, 4 or 8 or more.

MORE TOOLS

This kind of project is easier if you have a few mechanical drawing tools: a drawing board, a T square, a triangle (30-60-90°), a pair of dividers.

Also: black india ink, small jar of white tempera, and No. 1 watercolor brushes for each. Rinse the brushes in a water jar and wash in soap and water at the end of the day.

Designing your newspaper—what size?

You can put out a 4-page paper by folding a sheet of paper in half. The size depends on the sheet you use. You can also staple together single sheets.

If your printer has 11 × 17 inch paper, use it this way—

Plan where important news will go, where you'll have advertisements, announcements, and sports.

An 8½ × 11 inch sheet will make a mini-newspaper—

An 8½ × 14 sheet will give you room for two columns—

Making the paste-up sheet

On your drawing board, tape a piece of paper the size of one newspaper page. Be sure it is lined up with your T square:

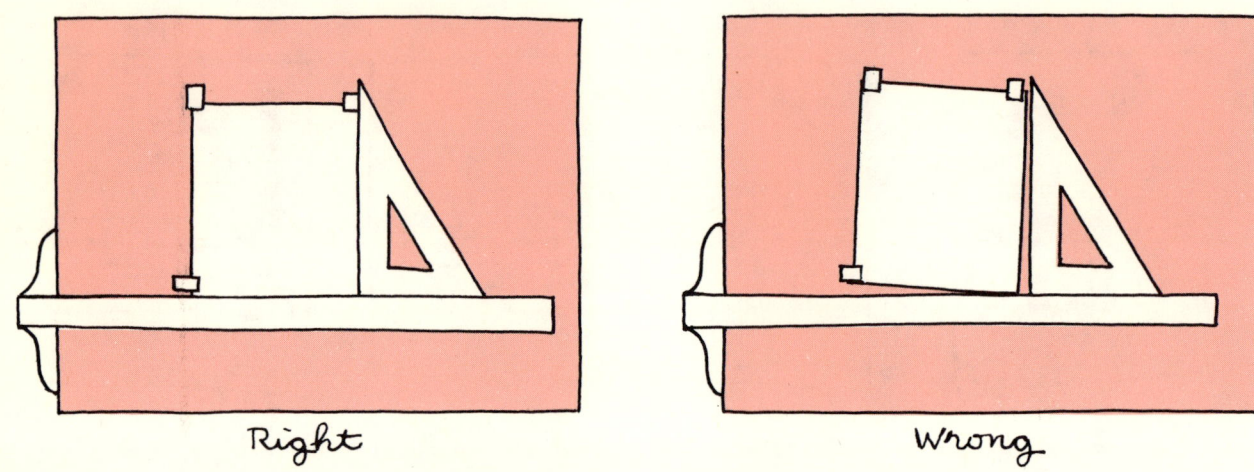

Right / Wrong

Draw a blue pencil line all around the sheet, 1/2 inch from the edges. Keep all type and pictures inside this line.

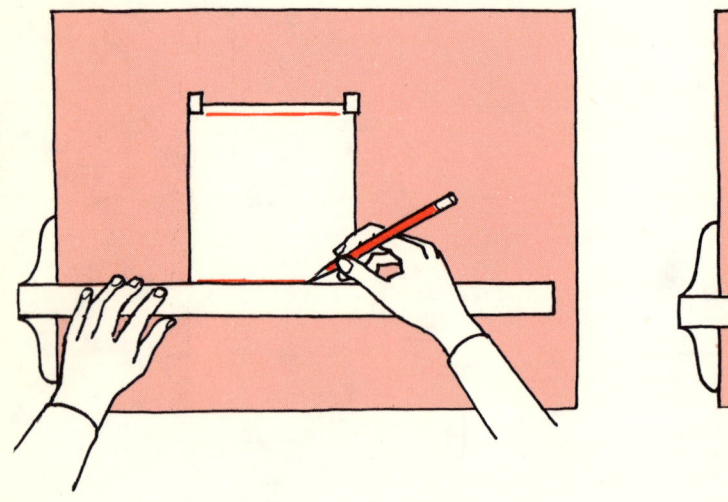
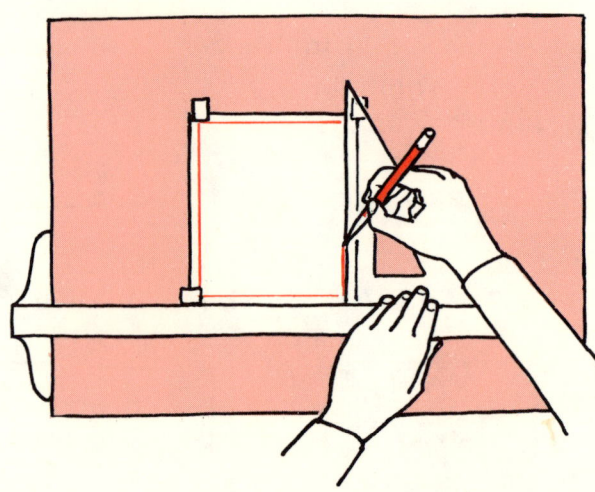

The masthead

Now make a masthead for your paper. You will use this title over and over, so make rough sketches until you have something you really like and won't tire of.

Sketch this on a clean sheet of paper, then go over your drawing with pen and ink or a felt-tip pen. Use clip art if you like.

The letters can be drawn by hand or taken from lettering sheets or letters cut from papers or magazines.

PROJECT 5/ NEWSPAPER, MAGAZINE, OR NEWSLETTER

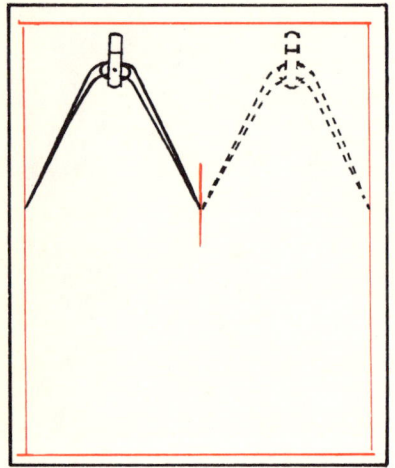

If you are going to have a 2-column page, find the center of the paste-up sheet and draw a blue line on each side of it. To find the center use the dividers or ruler or use the helpful hint below.

Preparing stories for paste-up

Draw two blue lines on a sheet of paper, one column width apart. If you can use a typewriter, type the story between the lines. Clean the typewriter keys first, and use a good ribbon and smooth paper.

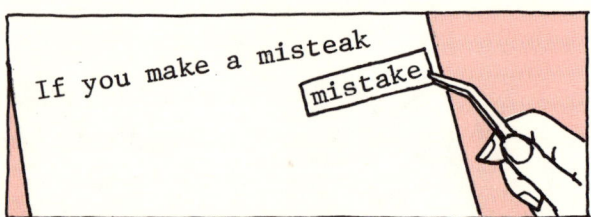

If you make a mistake, type a new word or line and cement it over the mistake.

You can hand-letter the stories, using a black ball-point pen or fine felt tip. Draw blue lettering guidelines with a T square.

HELPFUL HINT

How to find the center of a line or space with a strip of scrap paper:

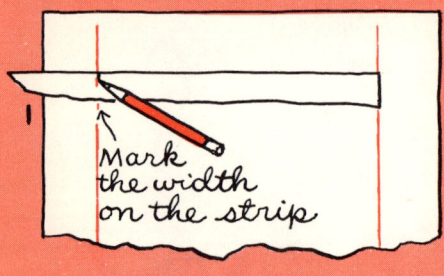

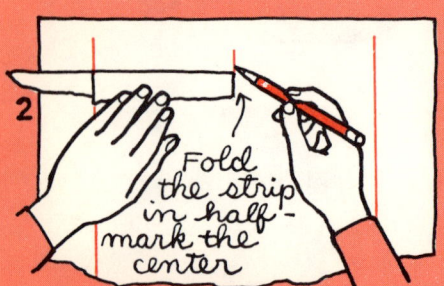

Find the center of a line of type the same way.

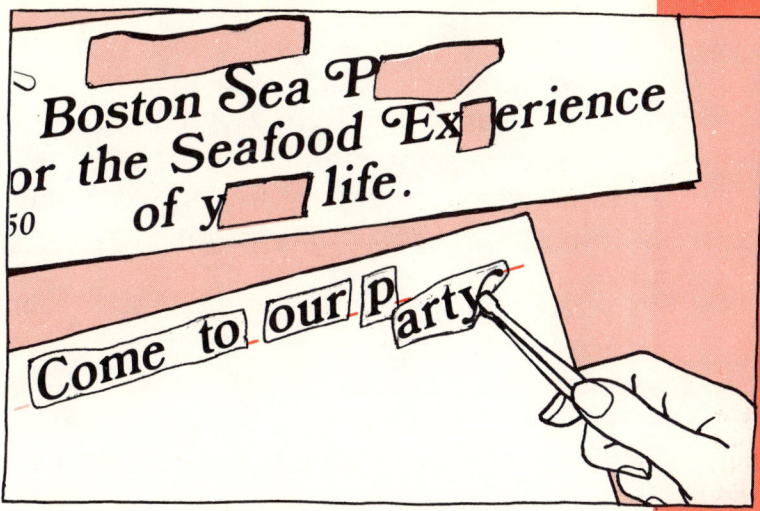

Putting your newspaper together

Each story needs a headline. Print it with a felt tip pen or cut out letters and words from newspapers or magazines, or use lettering sheets.

Newspaper headlines are lined up at the left—this is called "flush left" and is an easy way to make a good-looking page.

You can center headlines, too. Mark the center of your column and the center of each line of typing or printing. Center one line under the other, with equal space between lines.

Fit in the stories that go under your headlines.

Do you have space left over? You can draw pictures or decorations. Or use some of the clip art from your file.

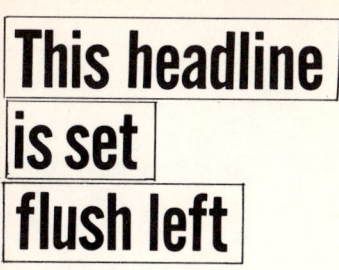

Headlines can be set either "flush left" or centered in

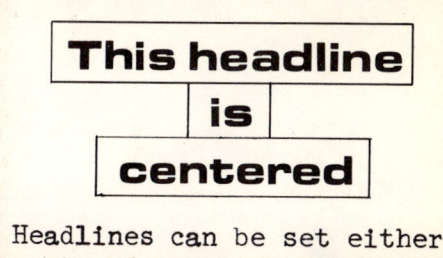

Headlines can be set either centered in the column or

Making everything stick

Lay all the pieces in place on your paste-up sheet. When you have your headlines and stories and art arranged to suit you, mark lightly with your blue pencil where each part goes.

Set all the pieces aside. Tape your paste-up sheet in position on your drawing board. Now cement each piece into its place. You will want to use your masthead again, so cement it lightly at the corners.

If you have a T square, use it to make sure you are getting lines straight on the page.

Clean up with a kneaded eraser and ball of rubber cement. Cover any unwanted marks with white tape or tempera.

Do each page of your paper the same way. Be sure to put a number on each page so that the printer will get them in the right order.

Congratulations! Your first paper is ready to go to press.

PROJECT 5/ NEWSPAPER, MAGAZINE, OR NEWSLETTER 43

BEACON ST. BUGLE

10 cents   May

Puppet Show May 7

NORBERT CLARENCE KOOKY
Stars of the puppet show

A musical comedy extravaganza will be presented Saturday night, May 7. The stars of the gala show are the Tyler Puppets, creations of Helen and Jimmy Tyler.

The show is being sponsored by the Monroe School PTA and will be presented in the school auditorium at 8 PM. Admission is $1.50 for adults, 75¢ for kids. Refreshments will be available.

Put out trash Saturday for alley clean-up

Is an old bed bugging your basement? Doesn't that beaten-up tan suitcase suit you any more? Want to get rid of those old venetian blinds?

Then don't pass up your once-a-year opportunity to clean out your basement and attic this Saturday. That's when the Harrison

(Continued on page 2)

FLASH!
Hank Carlson's cat George had six kittens Friday. George???

Enter your garden in the Garden Show!

Send this entry form to
The Garden Committee
85 Rand St., Geneva, OH 43210

I wish to show my garden
at_____
Name_____
Phone_____

1

PICK-UP (continued from Page 1)
Street Block Club, in cooperation with the city sanitation department, stages the annual pick-up of larger unwanted items.

Pick-up will start at 10:30 AM, so have all your unwanted things in the alley by that time.

Try to avoid overlaps

Lines like this can be drawn on the paste-up sheet

If a story is too long to fit on one page you can do this

Cover unwanted lines and marks with white tape or paint

To remove a stuck-down piece, loosen a corner and drop a little rubber cement thinner behind it.

PROJECT 6 Books

You can publish an ABC book, a coloring book, comics, or riddles—any short book you'd like. Decide on the page size, as large as 8½ × 11 or as small as 3½ × 4¼ inches. You can get a 16-page tiny book out of one 8½ × 14 inch sheet printed on both sides. (An 11 × 17 sheet makes 16 pages 4¼ × 5½.) Fold the dummy this way:

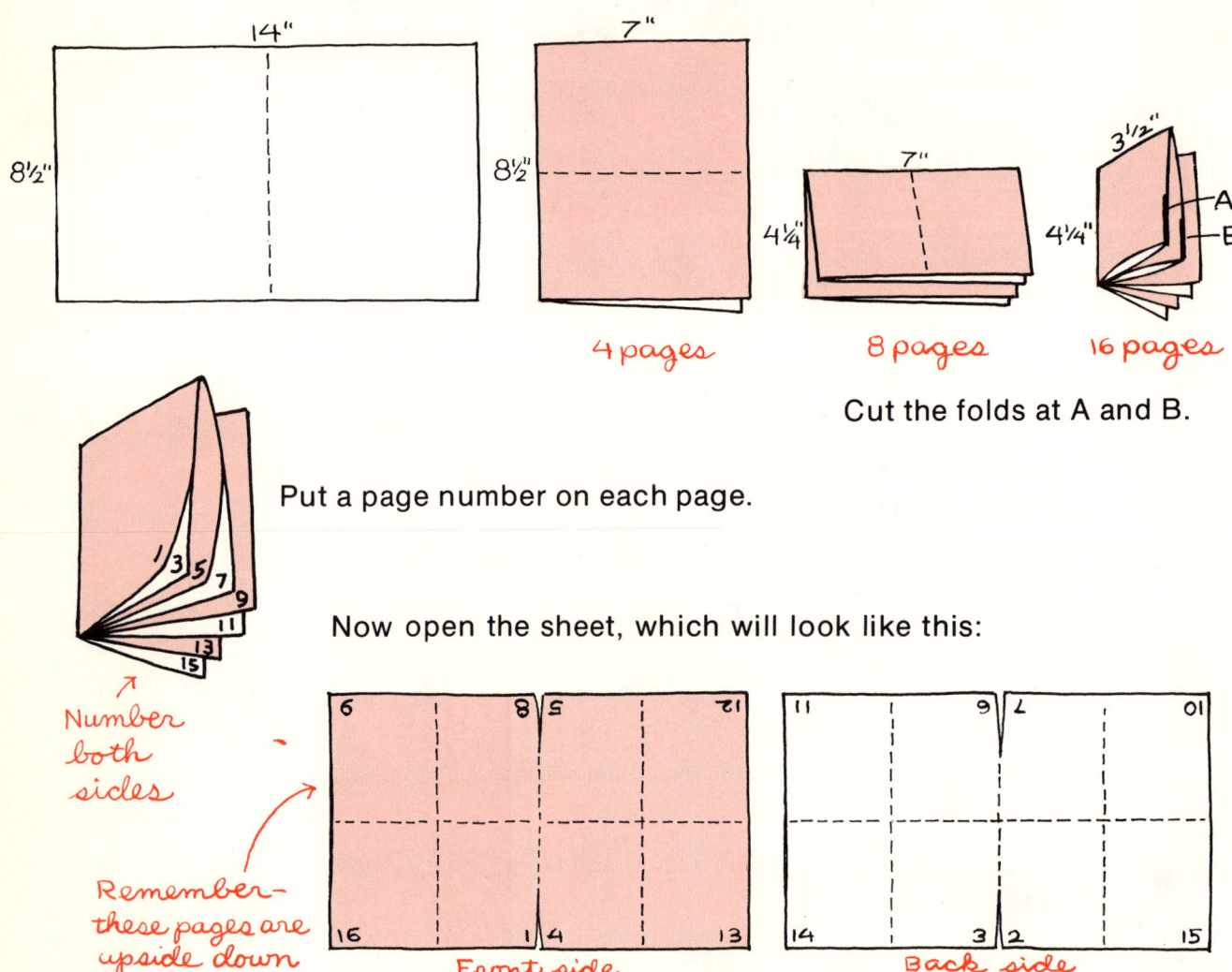

Cut the folds at A and B.

Put a page number on each page.

Now open the sheet, which will look like this:

Make your paste-up to fit this layout.

PROJECT 6/ BOOKS 45

Making the finished art

Plan your book to fit the number of pages in your dummy. Page 1 will be the title page. Start your story on page 2 or 3.

Make each page of finished art on a separate sheet and cement it in its proper place on the paste-up sheet. Allow at least 1/4 inch margin on each page. (Remember you'll need one paste-up sheet for each side of the page.)

Give the printer a dummy (use a copying machine to make duplicates of your finished work) so that your two sides of the sheet will back each other up correctly.

Fold your sheets and trim the top, bottom, and front edges. Add a cover of heavier colored paper and bind with a colored string or staples. Add color with markers or crayons to make your books attractive.

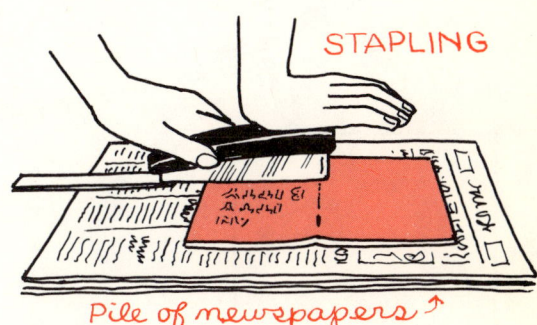

STAPLING

Pile of newspapers ↑

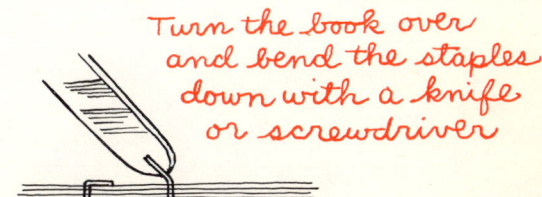

Turn the book over and bend the staples down with a knife or screwdriver

46 PROJECT 6/ BOOKS

↑ Clip art initial with hand lettering

More Book Ideas

How about making a "Night Before Christmas" book with cartoons of your family for a greeting card? Or write your own poem or greeting.

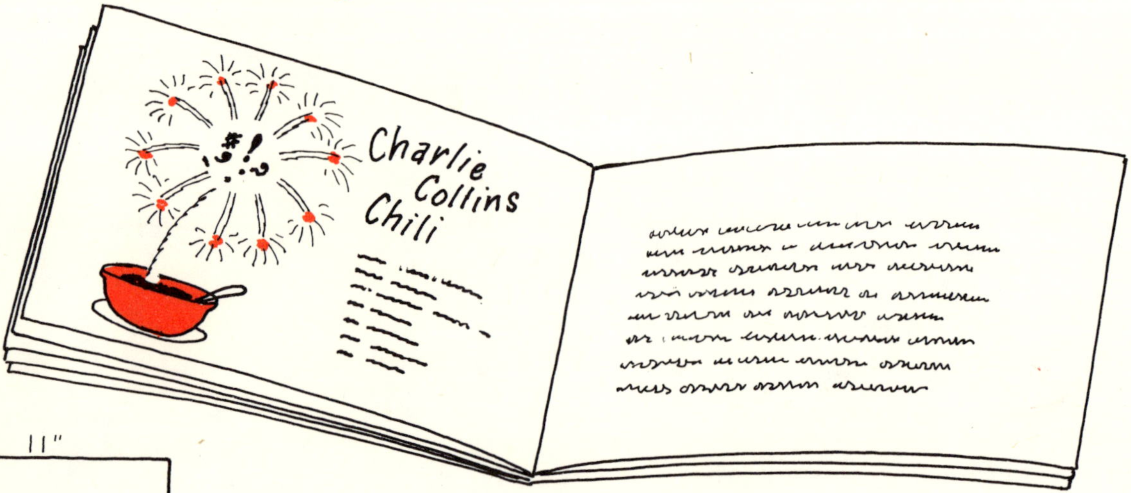

Print a recipe book for a club to sell. To make this long shape, fold an 11 × 17 inch sheet this way:

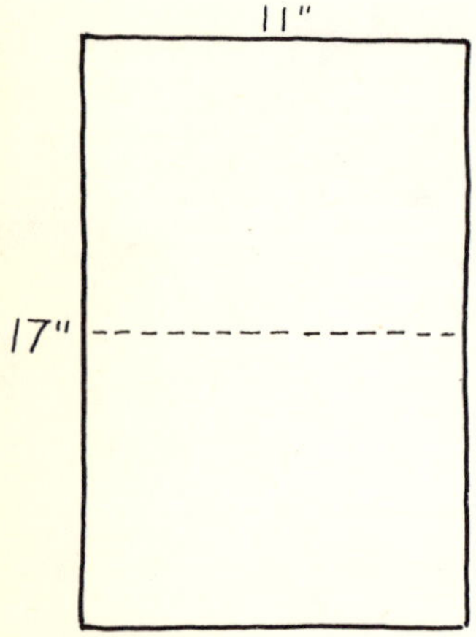

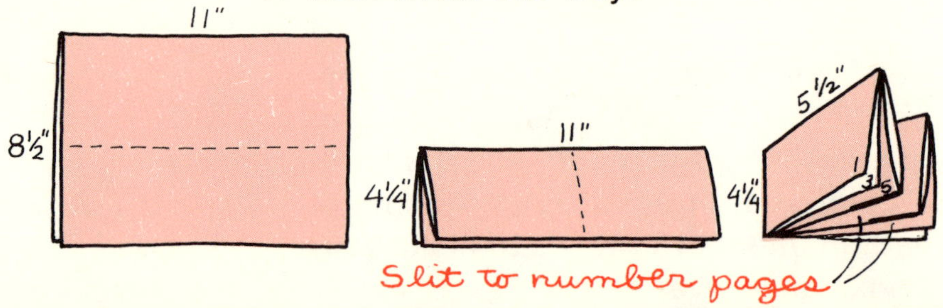

Slit to number pages

PROJECT 6/ BOOKS 47

Make a riddle book. Everybody loves riddles and they're not copyrighted. Put the answers upside down on the page or at the back of the book.

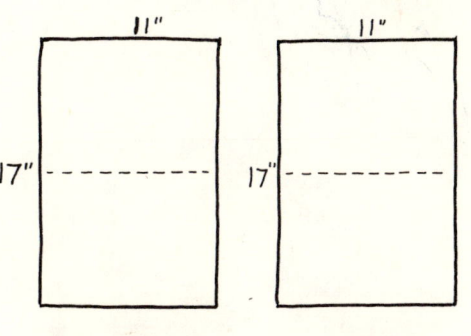

If you want larger pages, use two 11 × 17 inch sheets:

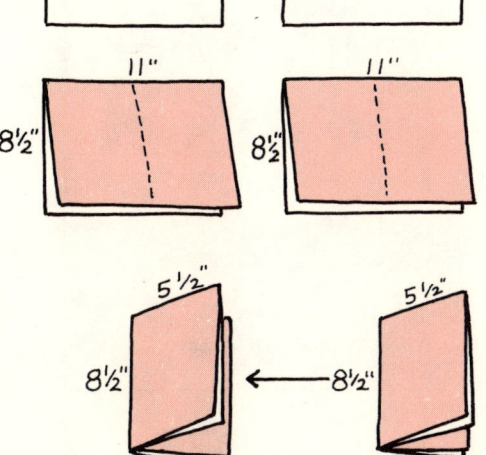

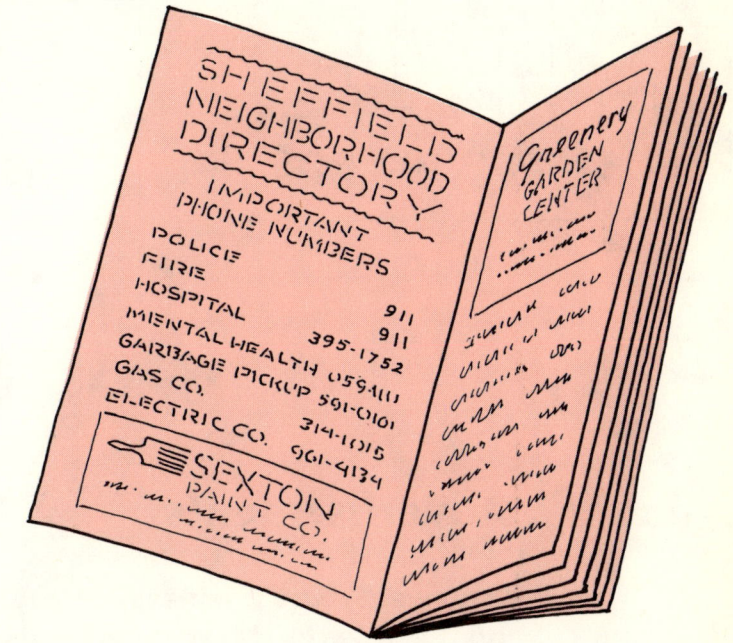

A neighborhood directory is another good idea. Sell ads to pay for the printing.

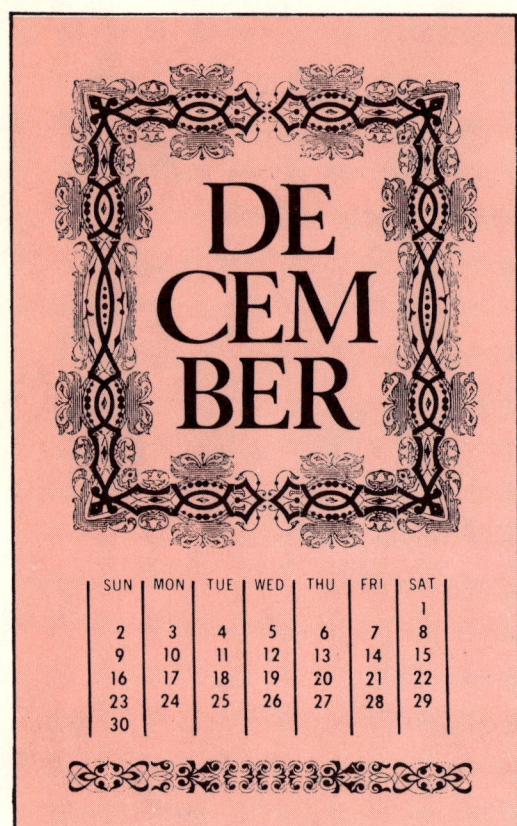

PROJECT 7 A Calendar

Everybody needs a calendar. Clip a printed calendar for the months and add original or clip art decoration. You might make sketches of well-known neighborhood places.

PROJECT 8 Advertisements

If you want more business, let your friends and neighbors know about your work. Make an advertisement to hand to people or to mail. Show off what you can do with design and imagination.

Sale ads, programs, small school posters—there are many kinds of printed pieces you can make for fun and profit. One job leads to another and new possibilities will open up for you.